D1540493

Bearing Fruit

A Child Learns About the Fruit of the Spirit

"The fruit of the spirit is love, joy, peace, patience, kindness, goodness, faithfulness, gentleness, self-control."

Galatians 5:22, 23

Bearing Fruit was written to help children: (1) to see and to enjoy the unique differences among physical fruits, and (2) to introduce young minds to God's characteristics (fruits) that are to grow and develop within each of us.

 A BEAR HUGS BOOK ™

Love Bears All Things: A Child Learns to Love

Bear Up: A Child Learns to Handle Ups and Downs

Bearing Burdens: A Child Learns to Help

Bear Buddies: A Child Learns to Make Friends

Bearing Fruit: A Child Learns About the Fruit of the Spirit

I Can Bearly Wait: A Child Learns Patience

Titles in Preparation:

Bears Repeating: A Child Learns Thankfulness

You are Beary Special: A Child Learns Self-esteem

Bear Necessities: A Child Learns Obedience

Bear Facts: A Child Learns Truthfulness

Bearing Good News: A Child Learns to Be Positive

Sweeter Than Honey: A Child Learns the Golden Rule

Copyright 1987, Paul C. Brownlow
Hardcover, ISBN: 0-915720-62-0
Library Edition, ISBN: 0-915720-64-7

Brownlow Publishing Company, Inc.
6309 Airport Freeway, Fort Worth, Texas 76117

Bearing Fruit
A Child Learns About the Fruit of the Spirit

By

Pat Kirk & Alice Brown

Illustrated by

Diann Bartnick

BROWNLOW PUBLISHING COMPANY, INC.

God makes fruit grow ripe and beautiful in His golden sun. Who else can make fruit grow...? No one! God has a plan for fruit to grow. It isn't just for pleasure or for show. It is a tasty treat for us fruit lovers — you and me. Yum!

What is your favorite? Red apples, tart and round? They hang green and gracefully from orchards all around. They start out little, then, before you know, they grow bigger and rounder as they ripen and grow.

Then...plop! The apples get too heavy for branches to hold. They drop to the ground—all ripe, red and round. Just right for the fruit bowl!

Cherries, too, are red and round, but they are much smaller little fellows. They cling together in groups of two or three. Just think of it. Let's gobble them in handfuls. There are enough cherries for both you and me!

Strawberries are ripe and red. They look like little triangles with green leaves growing right from the tops of their heads! They sit on the ground in little berry beds—not trees. And they're covered all around with tiny yellow seeds.

The huge green watermelon looks like a blimp. Next to it, the strawberry's a shrimp! Inside, the big melon is full of black, flat seeds and red, fruity mush. So dig in and eat all you can. But don't get in a rush!

Goodness comes in red all right. But it also comes in purple. Eating a cluster of juicy, sweet grapes is not a bit of trouble. Pick some from a vine anytime. Who cares that the little round balls go "squish" when you eat them? Licking juice from your lips makes eating grapes even more fun.

Does fun come in an orange, as bright and round as
a setting sun? You bet, it does! Start at the top and pull
one to see what you've unspun!

What fruit story could be complete without talking
about the blushing peach? It's fuzzy and fun to touch.
But when it is still on the tree, it's out of our reach!
When it does get ripe, all rosy and golden, let's be
there to catch it. And let's do more than just hold one!

Pineapples are a funny fruit. Who but God would dream of making a fruit with prickles like "whiskers" all around? It has spike leaves that shoot from the top and seem to say, "No touching allowed."

Who would guess such sweet, juicy fruit could hide inside? Just cut off the spikes and eat all you like — down to the core. It's really no chore!

Yes, fruit is pretty in color and shape. It has delicious flavors. Fruit smells tease your nose and make you lick your lips and wish you had some. And the taste is even better than the smell.

Yet, there is another story to tell.

There are special kinds of fruit created by God —
the fruit of God's spirit. But they don't grow on vines,
bushes, or trees. They grow inside you and me. The
seeds from this special fruit begin to grow when we
listen to God's word and obey Him.

These words become thoughts planted in our hearts and minds—just like fruit seeds that sprout in good, rich soil. God's germ of life begins to grow in our lives a little at a time.

Let's look at the collection of God's spirit fruit. We can't find them in our refrigerators or pantries. But we can taste them fresh from God's word—the Bible.

Love is the first and most delicious fruit in God's garden. God loved us first and told us so in His word. He even sent His own Son to earth to teach us how to love.

We all enjoy God's love every day. We can show God how much we love Him by loving ourselves and other people. Yes, love really is delicious.

Joy is the second fruit on the fruit shopper's list—
but not second best!

Joy is that happy feeling that comes to you when you know that you are important to God. You belong to Him. He is taking care of you. He has special plans for you as you grow up. He has special plans for all nature —people, plants, animals, earth and space.

Peace is the next fruit on the list. But it can't be bought at a grocery store. We can "taste" peace by trusting God. We know that He is helping us to grow every day to be just what He wants us to be. We don't worry about the weather or pests or anything else. We do our best. God does the rest!

Patience is a fruit that can grow only with prayer and
practice. Every fruit has its own season. God knows
what is best for us and He knows the right time to give
us everything we need. We ask — then relax!

Kindness and goodness are twin fruits of God's spirit —truly two of a kind. They are a delicious treat to eat and never bruise or spoil. Munching worms can never find a home inside them.

Both kindness and goodness are always on the side of right. They are happy for those who are happy. But they are also willing to share their delicious taste and aroma with someone who is sad. Who can do without kindness and goodness on their daily menu?

Faithfulness is a spirit fruit that must ripen in all God's children. This simply means that we never give up on ourselves or God. We trust His people, too. But

we are happy to forgive others when they make mistakes.

We cheerfully do what God wants us to because we love Him. We expect Him to help us to become the people He has promised to make us. So…we never quit or give up!

Gentleness is a mellow fruit. It uses its stored energy wisely. It releases just the right amount at the right time and in the right way. It is never bitter or sour like the taste of a sour lemon. It "goes down" smoothly. It treats people, animals and our entire universe with respect.

Self-control is a fruit that will never spoil. It will always be served for breakfast, lunch, dinner and in-between meal snacks! It is always needed. Self-control makes us think before we talk or act. Then we do only the things which help God, other people, and ourselves.

Bearing God's special fruit is not magic. But only God can produce it in us with our help. We will become happy, useful people as we live our lives to please God each day.

So help yourself to God's special fruits, anytime. Serve them to others. Then you will always appeal to God and He will make you the "pick of His crop."